Fashion Dolls

A Step-by-Step Guide
to Face Repainting

by Sabrina Guidice

Published by Hobby House Press, Inc.
Grantsville, Maryland
www.hobbyhouse.com

Dedication

Dearest Symba:

Even though your life was short, you were as regal, proud and beautiful as the "Lion King" that you were named after. You were the most loveable, affectionate, sweet little guy that anyone could ever hope for in a pet. We all miss you terribly. We will all always love you.

It was a shock to lose you - and even though you were mom's cat it's hard not to be with you and I'll never forget you. You have brought me so much joy in the time we were together. Your presence in my life has taught me some things I

needed to learn. Thank you for that and for sharing your loveable self with us all. You are always with me in my heart and you always will be. I love you Simmy. Rest in peace and happiness with all the kitty angels in Heaven. xoxoxoxo

Acknowledgements

To my family who helped support me through another book, thank you so much for being there for me. For everyone at Hobby House Press who believed in my books enough to give me the chance to prove myself, thank you for the opportunity. To Trouble, Bear, Sweetie and Symba, you guys are the reason that I exist - I couldn't have done it without my feline and canine "children" and to nanny of course, I wouldn't be who I am without carrying you everywhere in my heart. I love you and thank you all.

"Gene" is a trademark of Mel Odom and is used with his permission. Each of the dolls pictured within is the subject of a copyright owned by Mel Odom or Ashton-Drake, Inc. All rights reserved.

Additional copies of this book may be purchased at $19.95 (plus postage and handling) from
Hobby House Press, Inc.
1 Corporate Drive, Grantsville, MD 21536
1-800-554-1447
www.hobbyhouse.com
or from your favorite bookstore or dealer.

Printed in the United States of America

ISBN: 0-87588-646-9

Table of Contents

Artist Foreword

Hello everyone! It's fantastic to "see" all of you again! For those of you who know me, welcome to this next installment in the Creating Fashion Dolls series! For those of you who may not yet be familiar with my first book, congratulations! What you are holding in your hand is a truly unique book and a tool that will empower you creatively.

Whether you are a beginning artist of one-of-a-kind dolls, or a more seasoned professional, you will see that inside these pages are wonderful tricks and techniques revealed for everyone. My name is Sabrina Guidice and I'm an artist of one-of-a-kind fashion dolls, or as it is more affectionately known in the artist circles, an artist of OOAK fashion dolls. I would like to take this opportunity to tell you a little about myself, this book and the wonderful craft in which you are about to endeavor.

Growing up in Brooklyn in New York City in the 80's decade of decadence, celebrities and icons that have grabbed my attention and helped shape my life were not being represented in the dolls that were available. One day, I created a doll myself in the likeness of a famous person whose life I was fascinated with. As per a friend's suggestion and purely on a lark, I listed that doll on eBay™. When it sold for $200 overnight, I realized that a lot of other folks were interested in these one-of-a-kind dolls as well! It was obvious that there was a market for my work, and a fashion doll makeover artist was born!

I have been heavily involved in this niche market since that first endeavor selling my creations to collectors all over the world. I went on to write magazine articles and had my own column for a time. In addition, I run an online support group for other artists in this field. Thus, it is from my experience and that of fellow artists that the ideas for my books are born. I have always catered to the new artist, having taught online classes for a time. Information is hungrily sought after and many newbies to the field of one-of-a-kind dolls often pose questions to my online group regarding how to perform certain techniques on their own doll projects. In order to be a successful artist of OOAK dolls, artists no longer have to go through the trials and tribulations, failures and learning experiences that I had to go through back when I started. Information was not readily available regarding this craft at that time, but now through this series of books, you can learn solid skills and techniques as well as eye-opening tricks of the trade. With patience and practice you can learn to re-make fashion dolls professionally for show or for sale. Holding true to form, this book is written in a user-friendly manner just like my original book <u>Creating Fashion Dolls</u>.

<u>Creating Fashion Doll Repaints</u> is a necessary book. Teamed with <u>Creating Fashion Dolls</u>, you are armed with the weapons that you need to create some gorgeous one-of-a-kind dolls. On its own, <u>Creating Fashion Doll Repaints</u> will

teach you to paint doll faces like a true expert. There is so much information packed inside this book that I don't expect you to digest it all in one sitting. As with my previous book, there are plenty of full color pictures accompanying the step-by-step text instructions, which make this book easy to follow and easy to use. My books will show you the secrets and the techniques so that you as an artist can incorporate them into your own designs and branch out to create whatever your heart desires. In this book, I use the Gene® doll because she is large and the face is much easier to paint with true detail. Some of the techniques in this book can certainly be transferred to the smaller dolls, but most of the techniques were meant for the larger dolls because the repaints are more realistic on them and details are more evident.

I laid out this book the same manner as <u>Creating Fashion Dolls</u> by showing the step-by-step method of doing one repaint from beginning to end. If you look at the table of contents you can see that I cover everything that you need to know to create a gorgeous facial repaint by the time you finish this book. Beginners start at the beginning as I have just stated, but advanced artists may want to skip around and read the chapters of particular interest to them. This book is for everyone!

Starting with a conversation of the color wheel and the primary and secondary colors, we get a feel for mixing and creating truly one-of-a-kind shades to use on dolls that make them even more unique and difficult to duplicate! We go on to discuss materials and what you should have on hand in your workbox as a repaint artist and where to obtain these materials. Then I give you an in depth step-by-step instructional on how to create realistic eyes, lips and features. Furthermore, I include a very special chapter on using Milliput® paste with the help of artist Juan Albuerne. This chapter caters to the artist who wants to change the face shape or sculpt of a doll in order to resemble a celebrity, a real life person, or to simply change the original canvas doll to look completely different from all the rest. You also get to see some of Juan's most infamous celebrities in transition! Wow! In addition to all this, there is a chapter on specialty painting as well as a gallery of different facial expressions and looks that you can duplicate on your dolls. Ending with a great source section, this book is an incredible compilation of information!

So, grab a cup of coffee or tea, curl up and get ready to be enlightened! I'm sure much of what you are about to read will fascinate and inspire you, but again, please remember that anything worth doing takes time to learn and practice makes perfect. As the saying goes, good things come to those who wait and this is no exception. Don't expect to be a professional artist overnight. This book isn't magic, but it will enable you to develop skills in order to hone your talent and get better each time you practice a technique. Most of all, expect to have fun doing it and eventually you will create some magical dolls!

Good luck and happy re-painting!
~Sabrina Guidice

Chapter 1

Materials

What makes a good workbox? That is the question that we will answer in this chapter. There are certain items that are nice to have in your workbox but unnecessary. As you become more proficient in your craft and have mastered the skills taught in the coming chapters, you can go on to incorporate more expensive, advanced products into your workbox - especially if you are making money on your art. For now and for the sake of learning, I would ask that you start with only the basics and learn what I'm teaching before graduating on to other products. There are products though, that I feel would benefit a more advanced artist and I have marked those with a bold "A" to distinguish those items from the basics.

Let's break down everything you should have in your workbox. I will describe the items and why you need to have them. I am telling you what I use because I have experience with these products and I know they work. I have listed sources where you can find these items at the back of the book.

BRUSHES

Brushes are a critical part of what you are going to use to create your fashion doll repaints. They are every bit as important as the paint. Brushes come in a variety of sizes and brands. Sizes 3/0 to size 0 are ideal for this usage. I use size 0. They are among the smallest, thinnest paintbrushes I can find. I buy them from Dick Blick® and they are packaged in a set of 3 brushes.

Set of three size 0 brushes from Dick Blick®.

PAINT REMOVERS

Removing the paint from the face of a doll can be quite difficult depending upon the doll used. The original facial screening of the Gene® doll is stubborn to say the least and I have heard differing stories on whether or not pure acetone will ruin the vinyl on the doll later on down the road. I have always used nail polish remover WITH acetone. I feel that it is a happy medium between pure acetone and nail polisher remover with no acetone in it at all. You will need to decide which method to use according to your own judgement. Again, I am only stating what I use and that there may be a risk to using pure acetone. I also keep a variety of nail files and buffing blocks on hand. Nail files help scrape away original facial paint that will not come off with the nail polish remover while the buffing block helps to keep the surface smooth when I'm done filing.

Nail polish remover with acetone, buffing block, and bendable nail file.

PALETTES

A palette in my opinion is a necessity for any painter. Why? Because it is a structured element that helps keep paints separated especially when learning how to mix them. Small plastic palettes are my choice because they are inexpensive. I like to make cleanup as easy as possible so I cover the palette in tin foil and press it into each depression in the palette. By doing this, you can mix paints and then strip the foil off afterward so you do not have to scrub the paint off your palette. Furthermore, this is a good way to save paint that you may want to use again. Just fold up the foil to keep the paint free from dust. Then, when you're ready to use it again, just wet it down and mix well.

Palette covered in aluminum foil.

ACRYLIC PAINTS

Acrylic paint is the best medium for repainting dolls. There is no need for the beginner artist to go out and spend a lot of money on various color paints. Instead, mix your hues from the primary colors as is taught in the next chapter. It will not only make you proficient in working with acrylic paint, but it will save money as well. This is what I am recommending you put in your workbox in the way of paint:

Liquitex® Pthalo Blue	Liquitex® Acra Crimson
Liquitex® Yellow Light Hansa	Liquitex® Mars Black*
Liquitex® Titanium White*	Liquitex® Umber**

Liquid paint: Mars Black, Titanium White, Yellow Light Hansa, Acra Crimson and Pthalo Blue.

Note 1* I always try to buy the larger tubes of black and white as they are two colors that get used more than any other. Black and white not only stand alone, but they are base colors used in mixing as well because they increase or decrease the value of other colors. Therefore, you will use more of these colors than others.

Note 2* Brown is perhaps one of the hardest colors to mix. I suggest that you learn how to mix earthtone colors one of which is brown, but you may not want to go through that process every single time you need a brown hue. Therefore, I suggest keeping a tube of umber on hand. That is the only extra color other than the primary colors that I suggest you buy for now.

SEALERS

Sealers are a matter of personal preference. To some artists, sealers are very important while others choose not to use them that often. It is basically up to you whether or not you would like to seal your work once it's done. When I start teaching you techniques in the coming chapters, you will see that I stress to use thin coats of paint and sealer in <u>multiple layers</u>. This helps prevent the paints and sealers from peeling and coming off. You will learn that this is not the case on every repaint you perform. Sometimes even when you do take the precaution to seal your work, it will chip, crack, fade or peel off depending upon the type of vinyl used in the doll, weather, humidity, age, handling of the doll and so forth. It is rare, but it does happen. Using sealers on your work does help to prevent accidents, but it doesn't guarantee anything. I personally use sealer to help safeguard my work, but I use it with the knowledge that it is not going to protect my repaints 100% of the time.

BLENDING MEDIUM

I have never used acrylic paint on canvas. When I paint on canvas, oil paint is my medium of choice because I paint with the wet-on-wet-technique. However, oil paint has no place on a doll's face. It is smelly, it takes forever to dry, and the oil-based pigment will mar the doll's vinyl in the years to come causing the paint to look like it is smudged or seeping into the vinyl. In the case of acrylics, if you are really new to handling them, you discover that they dry very quickly. That is why acrylic blending medium is so useful. Just because you are not painting on canvas does not mean that you cannot use the same techniques as an artist that does. Blending medium is great for several reasons. First off, it keeps the paint wetter longer so that you don't have to keep spraying the paint with water to moisten it. It also mixes with the paint resulting in a sort of "cloudy" appearance. This gives the paint a warmer and softer shade, which is great for using on a doll's face for things such as eye shadow and other areas of "cosmetic repainting." The last reason why blending medium is useful is because it stretches the amount of paint thereby saving money. For instance, you can mix a gorgeous color of purple and need several shades of it. By mixing half of your purple color with blending medium you will effortlessly get a variation on the original shade without having to waste paint by mixing more variations on a single color.

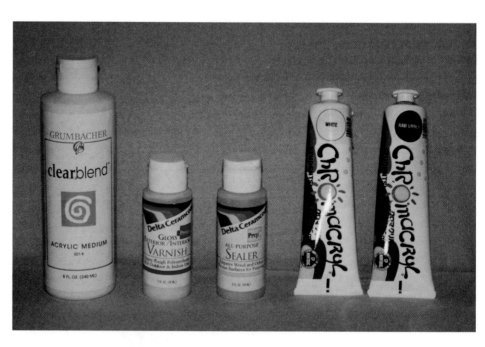

Grumbacker® acrylic blending medium
Delta Ceramcoat® sealers in gloss and matte
Chromacryl® acrylic paint in white and umber

ACRYLIC POT GLOSS PAINT (A)

I consider this an advanced artist's item because it's really not necessary. It is a luxury that you should only consider if you are making money from your work. Acrylic pot gloss paint, such as the ones shown here, can be expensive and are usually found in hobby and model shops. They are intended for use on model cars because they have such shine to them; but since they are acrylic, they can be used on vinyl. They are watery in texture and do not mix well, which is why they come in every color imaginable. They have an odor while you use them, but they do dry odorless.

Assorted Tamiya™ Pot acrylic paints.

NAIL POLISH (A)

Believe it or not, most people do not realize that nail polish is acrylic paint. I have used nail polish on my doll faces since the beginning of my career. They are odorless when dry as you know, and they come in many fabulous fashionable shades so premixing is not required. I do not suggest using nail polish colors all over your doll's face. What I do suggest is that you use nail polish only when you are trying to achieve a certain color that you cannot get by mixing paints. As a rule, nail polish is more prone to chipping than other acrylic paint, which is why you must seal it. I only use it in small areas when I'm looking for a particular color, such as a metallic eye shadow in an odd shade that I cannot find in paint or a super frosty lip color that I cannot reproduce by mixing paints

Assorted brands and colors of nail polish.

myself. I recommend that you be proficient in your repainting skills before attempting to use nail polish color because it can be expensive and nail polish formulas are meant to dry quickly. They are also much thicker than regular acrylic paint. Since you really can't water them down or mix them, you have to apply them more quickly than regular acrylics before they dry or clump. As you know, the only way to remove nail polish from any substance is with nail polish remover. Therefore, if you make a mistake due to the consistency of the paint and the speedy drying time, nail polish remover will undo the mistake, but it may also take off too much of the flesh tone from your doll's vinyl if you keep removing mistakes. Then the doll will be difficult or impossible to fix.

PENCILS AND CHARCOAL

Whenever you remove facial screening from a doll and are left with a literal blank canvas (face) to begin your repaint, it is extremely difficult to repaint the features freehand. So unless you are an extremely talented artist, don't attempt to do that. The reason artists of one-of-a-kind fashion dolls repaint faces is to get rid of the cartoon-like features that original facial screening tends to create. The idea then becomes to paint on more realistic natural-looking features. Therefore, you must sketch onto the canvas what you want your doll's face to look like. That is where graphite and charcoal pencils come in. We will discuss the techniques of sketching with graphite and charcoal later on in the techniques sections. I keep 2 graphite drawing pencils as well as 1 black and 1 white charcoal pencil in my workbox. I rarely use the white, but I keep it on hand in case there is an area that I absolutely want highlighted.

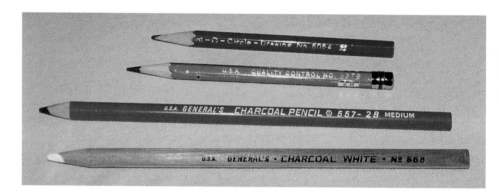

Graphite artist pencils, black and white charcoal pencils.

WATERCOLOR PENCILS

Watercolor pencils are an indispensable part of my workbox. They come in every conceivable color and work wonderfully on the Gene® doll's vinyl. I use them to draw anything I want to get a fine, thin line such as eyebrows, eyeliner, etc., as they offer more control than a paintbrush. The flesh tones are also used for emergency touch ups such as when my fingernail scratches the vinyl and I need a quick fix. Watercolor pencils are very tricky to use and must be used properly. They do stain the vinyl and tend not to come off when you try to "erase" the mistake, so please use them carefully and only where designated in our repaint course until you become more proficient. I was going to list these as advanced artist's tools, but then I realized that beginners can benefit from them as well for certain areas such as drawing in eyebrows, etc. If you are a beginner, get a small set of normal colors. Advanced users can buy the large tins of all colors such as the one pictured. Watercolor pencils are a nice way to use something other than acrylics for a totally different look or to incorporate with the acrylic paint for added dimension in the final look. Note that watercolor pencil features must be sealed, and the technique to seal them is very tricky. I will teach that in the coming chapters. Also, please keep in mind that watercolor pencils will work on some dolls, but not all.

Prismacolor® watercolor pencils.

MISCELLANIOUS PAINT ITEMS

Always keep an abundance of miscellaneous items in your workbox. I keep the following on hand at all times:

Cotton balls

Toothpicks

Dip sticks (I will show you how to create one of these later)

Paint mixers and orange wood sticks

Eye cotton swabs

Straight pins

Makeup wedges

Small pieces of rag

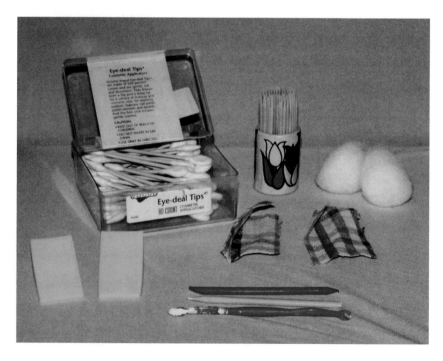

Eye swabs, cotton, toothpicks, makeup wedges, rag pieces, mixing and orangewood sticks.

EYELASHES

When creating a fashion doll repaint, one of the luxuries of changing a doll's features is to give her gorgeous lush eyelashes. That is like the proverbial icing on the cake. Painted on lashes are okay, but real lashes or rooted lashes are spectacular and are a detail that will set your dolls apart from the rest. Here is what I keep in my workbox:

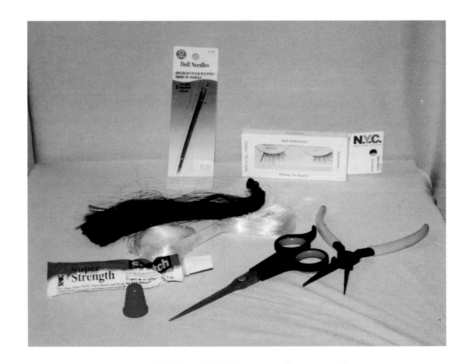

Doll needles
Faux women's eyelashes
Loose hair plugs
Scotch® brand adhesive glue
Thimble
Scissors
Needle-nose pliers

PUTTING IT ALL TOGETHER

If you read my last book, and are reading this book, you can surmise that there are certain places where I would not skimp on products for my dolls, but there are definitely times when being thrifty is smart. You can buy whatever your heart desires to hold all of these items in place for you. You can spend a lot of money on a customized or a specialty box to keep your items in or you can reuse something that you would have normally tossed into the trash! My workbox is not a box at all but a bag. The bag pictured contained a set of sheets. I didn't have a lot of money at the time I started my makeovers in 1998 and what money I did have, I spent on basic supplies. So when I removed the sheets from the bag, I was on my way to throw it in the trash when it occurred to me that it would make a great bag for my paints and other items. What I love about this bag is that it is made of reinforced plastic that is incredibly strong. It also has a zippered cover and a plastic pocket in the back where I keep my smaller items. This bag has been tossed, dropped, and smashed in a huge container with all the rest of my doll supplies, yet it doesn't have a hole, tear, or snag after all these years. I just never had a need to replace it! And the fact that it's clear really works for me because I can see what I'm pulling out without removing all the contents. It is compact, but as you can see, it holds a great number of items. As a matter of fact, most of the previous items shown are inside this bag!

Once you have your workbox (bag) assembled, proceed to the next chapter to learn how to work with color!

Chapter 2

Working with Color

Color definitely makes a strong statement! To me, color is one of the most fascinating things in our world. Look at nature for a moment — the wildly vibrant colors of flowers, the peaceful serene colors of our skies and waters. Look around at your fellow man and all the wonderful colors we come in! Color can even affect our mood. Many wonderful artists use color as the epicenter of their work. Whether it is the dreamy abstract hues on a painter's canvas, the lushness and depth of brilliant color in a designer's fabric or the serenity or warmth of an interior designer's room—color conveys mood and creates a certain feeling or tone. This is true for the one-of-a-kind doll artist as well. Color plays a variety of roles from the color of the doll's skin tone and hair to the outfit that it wears. Perhaps the greatest depth of color will be those that appear on the doll's face. Here, I will teach you about color — how to understand it, create it, work with it, and use it to make your dolls "pop."

THE COLOR WHEEL

When working with tube acrylic paints, it is more cost effective for artists to be able to learn how to mix colors to create various hues instead of buying every single color he or she may need. Tube paints are the right consistency and texture for mixing. If you are using high gloss or specialty pot acrylics, then I would recommend buying the colors that you need rather than mixing them. Again, I suggest high gloss and specialty pot acrylics for the advanced artists only or for those artists who don't care if they make mistakes on their dolls. These paints are too thin to mix and oftentimes, will not come out properly. Getting back to our tube paints, I have provided you with a color wheel in this photograph.

Notice the circles that point to the 3 *Primary Colors*. The primary colors are red, yellow, and blue. These colors are called primary colors because they are the bases of every other color. You cannot create true red, yellow, or blue by mixing other colors together.

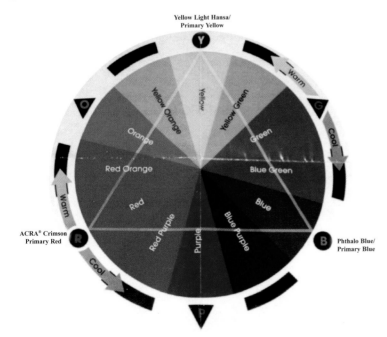

Notice the triangles that point to the 3 *Secondary Colors.* The secondary colors are orange, green, and purple. Notice on the chart the black lines that represent the *Intermediate Colors.* They are red orange and yellow orange, yellow green and blue green, blue purple and red purple. Secondary and intermediate colors are those colors that are created by mixing various amounts of red, yellow, and/or blue together. For instance, when you mix *equal* amounts of red and yellow together you get orange. Then you can create red orange or yellow orange depending upon the proportion of red and yellow. Red orange has *more red* than yellow whereas yellow orange has *more yellow* than red. This may sound confusing to you at first, but if you take a moment to digest this information, it makes perfect sense. Not only that, but it's necessary for you to be able to learn to mix colors properly and you will need to know these basics in order to go on with this chapter. By the way, you may have noticed that next to the primary colors on the color wheel you see names like Yellow Light Hansa, Phthalo Blue and Acra Crimson. These are the company names of the colors of Liquitex® acrylic tube paints that most closely resemble the primary colors of true red, yellow, and blue. They are there for your information should you decide to buy Liquitex® brand acrylics which I highly recommend.

COLOR CHARACTERISTICS

Hue is the actual color. Hue classifications are warm or cool as seen on the color wheel. Chroma is the intensity of color. Value is the lightness of a color and is adjusted accordingly by adding black or white.

EXAMPLES

A hue of red is classified as a warm tone and a hue of blue is classified as a cool tone. To adjust the hue of a color, mix it with neighboring hues on the color wheel. You can adjust the hue of red by mixing it with purple, orange, or yellow. You can adjust the hue of blue by adding purple, green or yellow, and so on. Successful color mixes use a minimum of colors - adding too many to a mix makes the color you are trying to achieve too dark or muddy. Since some colors are very strong, use judgment when mixing by eye, not by the amount of paint you are using.

You can decrease the intensity of a color by mixing it with its complementary color. Green will tone down the color red for instance. If you mix equal amounts of complimentary colors, you usually end up with brown. Again, use judgment by eye and not by amount of paint being put into the mixture. Sometimes, a little goes a long way.

If you want to make any shade that you've mixed lighter, add a little white to it. If you want to make it darker, add a little black to it. Again, a heavy hand will not work well here. You can always add more, but you can't take out what you've already added. Be sure to note this important fact, if you are in the midst of mixing a color and you add too much white making the color too light, adding black to darken it will not work. On the flip side, if you add too much black, adding white to lighten it will only make it look chalky. You would most likely have to start over again, so mix colors a little at a time.

EXERCISE

I am including a color wheel template here for you to enlarge and copy so as not to ruin your book.

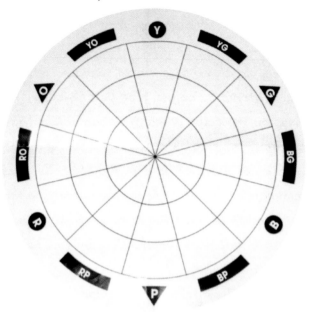

With what you have learned thus far, practice mixing the secondary colors and getting them to match as closely as possible with the shades on the color wheel pictured in the book. After you have achieved satisfactory secondary colors, I would like you to try toning down each primary color and then change the values lighter and darker. Remember that toning down the primary colors requires you to mix them with a complementary color as shown on the wheel and as discussed previously.

Once you have gotten a feel for mixing the secondary colors, print out another copy of the blank color wheel and try for the intermediate colors. These skills will last you a lifetime and if you are like many artists, these techniques will transcend any painting art form and will help you with your endeavors whether they be on canvas or anywhere you need to mix colors.

MIXING SHADES AND TONES

If you add black to any color, that color then becomes a "shade" of the original color. Mixing white and black together makes shades of gray. If you add gray to any color, that color then becomes a "tone" of the original color.

MIXING EARTHTONE COLORS

No matter what kind of painting artist you are, you will always need to use earthtone colors. As mentioned before, combining complementary colors will eventually create some shade of brown. Red mixed with green, blue mixed with orange, and purple mixed with yellow can make many different earthtone shades. Brown is perhaps one of the hardest shades to mix, but I don't want anyone to get overwhelmed and end up not mixing them. A good mixture to try is primary yellow with true purple, blue purple, or red purple. Also try true orange with primary blue, true green, blue green, blue purple, purple or red purple. Try red orange with blue green, true green, primary blue, blue purple or true purple. These will give you nice earthy colors.

While it may seem like a lot of work, once you get the hang of mixing colors, it is really easy. While I cannot possibly list all the color combinations and outcomes here, there are books that you can find in your local library, craft or bookstore that are dedicated to the subject of color and color mixing. What I have given you here is a basic plan that is laid out in simple terms so that everyone can understand the steps involved to successful color mixing.

There are many good reasons to learn this skill. Not only is it cost effective and important to your craft to learn how colors combine, but it is equally important because when you start to paint you will be VERY familiar with the feel and the flow of the paint. Acrylic paints dry quickly. If your paint dries before you're done using it, spray it with water to moisten it. An artist must know how his or her medium behaves and when you take control of mixing paints, you have an edge over other artists who choose not to get to know their medium.

You can practice on as many blank color wheels as you need to until you feel that you are savvy at mixing colors. Once you have this knowledge it will always serve you. Now, we are ready to remove that original facial screening on your doll and learn how to sketch in more realistic, natural looking features!

Acknowledgements I would like to thank and give credit to Liquitex® Corporation for their permission in reprinting their color wheel and color wheel template. Information on mixing paints was adapted from their color wheel insert, which can be found in some Liquitex® Acrylic starter kits. For more information on Liquitex® and their products, please see the contact information in the Sources section at the back of the book.

Chapter 3

Removing the Original Facial Screening

(Face Paint)

Most of the techniques used here work on other dolls as well; however, the screening on the original Gene® doll is especially durable thereby making it difficult to remove. Here I use the Simply Gene® doll in her original state. Make sure you take her earrings out and keep her hair tied back for now. We are only concerned with her face.

Simply Gene® original state.

FOR THE FOLLOWING SECTION YOU WILL NEED THESE ITEMS:

Doll minus any jewelry, hair tied back

2 small towels

Sheet of paper towel

Blow dryer

Tweezers

Nail polisher remover with acetone

Cotton balls

Dip stick (instructions to follow)

Bendable nail file

Buffing block

Water

REMOVING ORIGINAL EYELASHES

In order to remove the original facial screening from the doll, we start with the original eyelashes. Some artists prefer to leave the original eyelashes, but in my experience they are very difficult to work around so for the sake of this project, we will remove them. First, take a towel and wrap your doll's hair in it. Then wrap the remainder of your doll in the second towel. The purpose of this is to protect the vinyl and the hair during the process of heating the eyelashes with the blow dryer. Using the blow dryer, apply heat on a low setting. Be sure to aim the dryer directly at the doll's eyes. After a few seconds remove the heat and test the lashes with

Left: Wrapping hair and body in a towel.

Below: Applying heat to eyes.

the tweezers. Grip one corner of the lashes and pull gently. If they are still attached, apply more heat and test again until the lashes come off easily with the tweezers in one straight line. Gene® dolls are manufactured with glued on eyelashes and the glue that is used is particularly durable and stubborn to remove. The only way to get it off completely is to heat it in this manner.

Removing heated eyelashes with tweezers.

Repeat this process with the other eye. When you are finished removing both of the original eyelashes, your doll should look like the one pictured below. If there is stubborn glue residue remaining once you remove the eyelashes, simply try picking it off with the tweezers. Do not scratch the vinyl. This is why applying sufficient heat is so important. However, apply the heat in increments so that you do not melt your doll!

Original doll without original eyelashes.

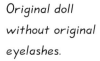

Buffing the filed
face smooth.

the doll until the face paint is removed entirely, and then using a
soft black buffer block, buff all the areas that you filed to maintain
the smoothness of the doll's vinyl. When you are finished with your
filing and all traces of original paint are removed, rinse the doll's
face under cool water and dry thoroughly with a paper towel. Even
now my doll still has some face paint remnants; however, the idea
behind the filing is to make sure that the surface is smooth and free
of any paint or glue lumps that might be evident on the doll or
would mar the finish when I am finished repainting. Again, if your
doll's face paint is stubborn and it doesn't look like much more of the
paint has come off, that's okay. You want to get as much off as
possible, but it really doesn't have to be completely paint free as
long as the surface is smooth.

Note As with anything new, these techniques take practice. If
you are afraid that you will ruin a more valuable doll with your first
attempts, practice on a less expensive doll until you feel that you
are ready to try something more valuable. Unfortunately, even with
practice there is no guarantee that you will not ruin your doll. I
have certainly ruined a handful of dolls in my day, but that is how
we learn — by our mistakes. There is no way around that, so just
relax and plan to invest some money in a couple of dolls before you
master the paint removal and filing techniques. After all, you can
always save money in other areas of creating your one-of-a-kind
doll.

Okay! So now we have our blank canvas doll. Study the face
for a moment to get a feel for the features. Now, let's move on to
judging the face shape and sketching in the new features for a
one-of-a-kind look!

Chapter 4

Studying Face Shape

Sketching with Graphite and Charcoal

Real woman's eye.

Look at this picture of a real woman's eye. Notice how the eyebrow looks. Notice where it starts and where it ends. Next, look at the shape of the eye. See the brow bone, the crease, the eyelid. Look at the iris and the different flecks of color that are so noticeable. Now look at the pupil and the flash of white reflecting the light. Do you see how the whites of the eyes look rounded? Look into the corner of the eye and see the pink flesh. Then look at the inner rim of the eye. Finally, notice how the eyelashes sit around the eye. This is what a real eye looks like. This is what you want to duplicate on the doll to the best of your abilities.

Look at this picture of the doll now, as a blank canvas. You have the original mold to work with if you want to follow that or you can get creative and change eye shape, lip shape, even nose shape and face

Blank canvas Gene®.

38

shape. For the sake of this project and this particular chapter, we are going to take this blank canvas doll and use the original mold as our guide. We won't change anything, but we will give this doll a more realistic look by painting in more natural looking eyes and lips. In later chapters, I will show you how to do some re-sculpting to change the features as mentioned above. For now, notice where the eyebrow should go, the eyelid, the whites of the eyes, the iris, the pink corners of the eyes, and study the mold of the doll. Your re-creation of the face must be in proportion with that of a real woman but on a smaller scale. So study the real eye and study the blank canvas and picture in your mind how you will reproduce your idea. Then move on to the next phase.

SKETCHING WITH GRAPHITE AND CHARCOAL

FOR THIS NEXT SECTION YOU WILL NEED:

Doll completely devoid of any makeup, thoroughly dry
Pencil sharpener
Graphite drawing pencil (an artist pencil, NOT a no. 2 pencil)
Black charcoal pencil

You begin by sketching a base onto your doll. Using a very light hand, begin to sketch in where the eyebrows will go with a graphite pencil. If you need an example of different eyebrows, here are some basic shapes for you to play with. Remember, all of these shapes can be duplicated onto your doll but they must be in scale with her face. Follow the photo of the real eye shown previously in order to draw the correct dimensions of each part of the eye. If you want it to look natural, an eyebrow should always start off at the inside corner of the eye, have a slight arch above the center of the iris, and then taper to a thin end not stretching past the outer corner of the eye. There are, of course, other ways to draw eyebrows that border on the unique or even whimsical as shown in the following illustrations.

NATURAL EYEBROW EXAMPLES

Average thickness,
tweezed look with an arch.

Very streamlined shape.
Traditional 1950's look
A La I Love Lucy!

Very thin tweezed
rounded look.

Bushy rounded look.

Very modern, thin tweezed
look with a high arch.

Very rounded, pencil look.
Very Marlene Dietrich.

EXPRESSIVE EYEBROW EXAMPLES

You might want to try to sketch these brows out on paper first to get a feel for them and figure out how to draw them. It is often easier to draw the eyebrow that is located on the side of the hand you use to write. As long as you use a light touch with the graphite pencil, any mistakes or misjudgments should wash off easily with a little water. Make sure the area is dry before you attempt to draw again. Once you have placed your desired eyebrows on the doll, be sure not to touch the area with your fingers, as you will smudge the graphite.

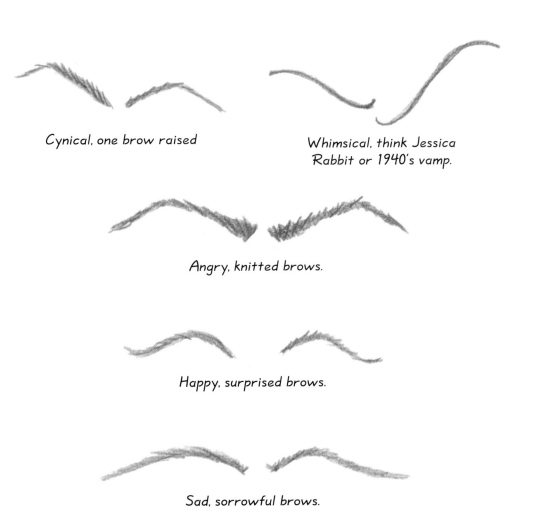

Cynical, one brow raised

Whimsical, think Jessica Rabbit or 1940's vamp.

Angry, knitted brows.

Happy, surprised brows.

Sad, sorrowful brows.

SKETCHING IN THE EYES

Refer back to this illustration of the eye as needed.

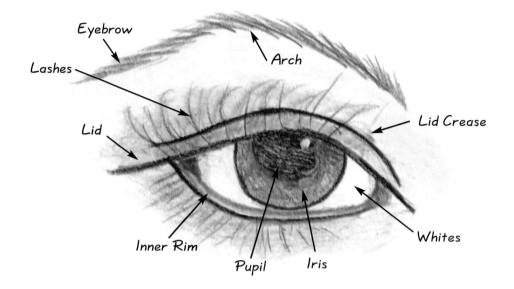

Believe it or not, it is typically easier to sketch the eyes than the eyebrows. This is because we are going to use the original doll's mold to guide us. To sketch the eyes, we need to enhance the shape of the doll's eye all around. Using the graphite pencil, sketch the shape onto the vinyl. Continue referring back to the photograph of the real eye while doing this. Keep in mind that the whites of a real human eye are round under the skin; therefore, when you begin to sketch eye shape, round out where the whites will be inside the "socket" before you draw the upper and lower lines of the lids around it.

Using graphite pencil, sketch the eye shape onto the canvas doll.

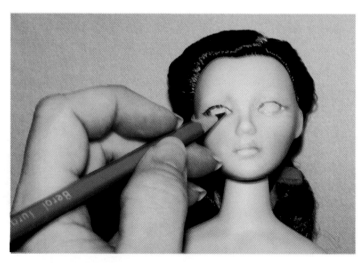

Next, draw a line between the brow bone and the eye lid of the doll to create the illusion of a crease. Again, use a light touch to sketch.

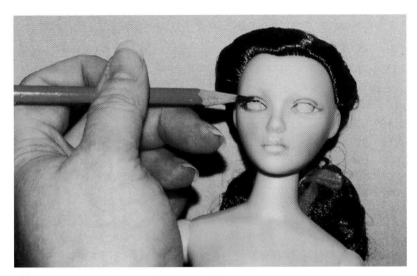

Drawing the crease.

Now look at the shape of the eye. Imagine that inside that oval is a white eyeball once again. Using the graphite pencil, ever so lightly, shade the inner and outer edges of the eyes to make the area appear 3 dimensional. Do not go so far into the inner corners of the eyes that you won't have any room to leave the pink flesh evident in a real eye. Just shade the edges where the whites of the eye would be. This will give your doll's eyes depth.

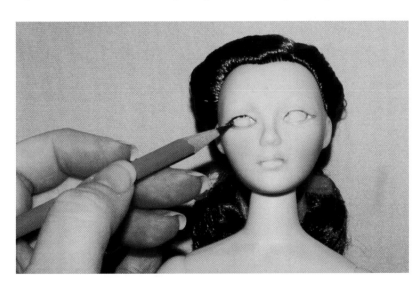

Shading the whites of the eyes for realism.

Next, put a circle where the iris will go in each eye — whether you choose to have side glancing eyes, eyes looking up, or down, or straight ahead is up to you. Just remember to have both eyes match exactly or your doll will look more like a cartoon character than a fashion doll. Then draw in a smaller circle inside the iris near the lid. This is where the pupil will sit in the eye.

Drawing in the irises and pupils.

Now, take a look at your doll. Look at the line on the bottom of the original oval that you drew to outline the shape. That line is going to become the shading area that will further define the whites of the eyes. Leave that line there. You are going to draw in another line right underneath that one leaving a smidgen of flesh toned vinyl between the two pencil lines. This is going to give the appearance of the lower rim inside the eye. Draw the second line from the inner corner to the outer corner of the eye on the doll according to the photograph of the real eye on the previous page. Then start to sketch in the little eyelashes along the lower lash line. Leave the top alone. Do not sketch eyelashes onto the top lid.

Creating the lower rim of the eye.

At this point you should also close up the area where the pink mound of flesh in each inner corner of the eye will be painted in. Do not shade this part however. We will be painting it pink later.

Add the sketched eyebrows after you decide what shape you desire.

Now, take your black charcoal pencil and sharpen it to a fine point. Sketch the area above the eye where you want your eyeliner to go. This will further emphasize the shape of the eye. Don't forget, the more you pronounce the features, the easier it will be to paint them in at the end.

Using charcoal to place eyeliner on the eyes.

At this point, your doll should look like the one shown here, completely sketched with eye brows and eyes. (see below)

SKETCHING THE LIPS

You can stay within the original confines of the mold for the lips or you can be a little adventurous and draw new lips to be colored in later without changing the structure of the mold or having to sculpt. Here are a few examples of different types of lips:

EXAMPLES OF LIP SHAPES

Average, natural lips.

1950's, I Love Lucy look.

Thin, shapely lips.

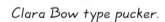

Clara Bow type pucker.

Bee Stung lips.
Full and pouty.

Thin upper
lip, full lower.

Upper lip with
no peaks.

Open mouthed smile.

Before sketching in your lips, decide which expression you are giving your doll based on the eyebrows and then sketch the appropriate lip shape for that expression. For example, if you are sketching mischievous eyebrows because that's the expression that you want your doll to reveal, then the lips may be a little "pulled" to one side as she gives a sideways grin. For example, look at my rendition of Jennifer Lopez from the movie *The Cell* that I created on a Gene® doll in the Gallery section. Notice how I sketched in a smirk on her face emphasizing the cheek area by shading in the expression and the shape of the lips. You will have to decide how you want the face to look before you actually sketch them onto the doll.

For the purpose of this book, I sketched in eyes that stare straight ahead with normal brows and full lips according to the mold. The extra information explained in this chapter is there for you to experiment and have fun.

Completely sketched face.

Now that your doll's features are completely sketched in, it should look similar to the one pictured here.

She's ready for color!

Now we are ready to move on and fill in some color!

Chapter 5

Repainting Realistic Features

REALISTIC EYES

Now that you have successfully sketched in the look that you want on your doll's face, you are ready to make that face come alive by repainting and adding color. As you will see in later chapters, the time to change structure on the face and to add expressions through shadowing and highlighting is when you sketch the face onto the doll with the graphite. Once you repaint the features onto the face, it is not wise to wipe the paint off and go for a different look so be certain of the following before you start to paint:

Is this the overall look that I want for my doll?

Is this the expression that I want for her face?

Did I sculpt her face enough to begin repainting? (Advanced chapter)

Is there anything else that I want to add before I begin to repaint?

After you've asked yourself these questions and are satisfied with what you have, you are on your way to finishing your repaint. The reason that you shouldn't remove the paint for a second time is because you risk discoloring the vinyl with stray paint or with the nail polish remover. Mistakes of that nature are often difficult to correct. Therefore, unless this is a practice doll, try to do it right the first time. Little mistakes can be fixed, but not an entire face full of paint!

TOOLS YOU WILL NEED FOR THIS SECTION

Your sketched doll

Glass of water

Pencil sharpener

Eraser (I use a typing eraser with a brush on the other end)

Nail polish remover

Paper towel or bits of rag

Dip sticks

Makeup applicators

Any size brush 3/0 or lower, 0 being ideal

Primary colors of Liquitex® acrylic paint

Tin of mixed color watercolor pencils

Palette covered with aluminum foil

2 Sealers, matte and gloss

Faux eyelashes

Scotch® brand adhesive

Scissors

Real women's oil free blush or eye shadow in pink and beige

Let's begin at the top. We will follow the guideline of the sketched area to:

REPAINT REALISTIC EYEBROWS

This part can be a bit tricky and for those of you who would rather use paint than the watercolor pencils, feel free to go ahead and do just that. However, I must warn that while you can wipe the paint right off if you make a mistake, using a paintbrush will not give you the control that the pencil will and it may take you several tries to get the eyebrow correct even with the outline already there. If you are going to use paint, be sure to mix a shade that is going to work with your doll's hair color unless you're going for something really out there in which case, it doesn't matter. However, if you want a realistic look, which is what I did here on my model, make sure that the eyebrow hair color matches the head hair color.

Use a watercolor pencil in a shade as close to the hair color as possible. I used a reddish brown color for my redheaded doll. Use the dry pencil to sketch all around the outside of the eyebrow that you sketched in with graphite. Do not color it in however. After sketching the shape of both brows, take a thin eraser and erase the graphite pencil from the brow area. Now use a very light hand and shade in the entire brow. If you were going for a flat brow look, you could use a heavier hand shading or wet the tip of the watercolor

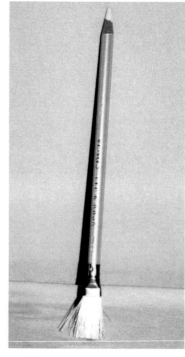

Clockwise:

Outlining eyebrows with watercolor pencil

Typing eraser.

Filling in brow area.

50

pencil and color in this area. Afterward, seal it. I like the look and attention that individual hair commands on my dolls and Gene® is certainly an appropriate scale for that. In that case, use a very light touch to shade the under layer of the brow and create the shape. Then, use the same pencil, and with a heavier hand, follow the shape of the brow and add individual lines following the pattern of natural hair growth. This will create dimension.

Complete individual hair brows.

Now you need to seal the area. Watercolor pencil is very tricky when it comes to sealing. It is true that when using the dry pencil on a doll's vinyl it tends to stain and be difficult if not impossible to remove. However, once you wet an area that you have colored with watercolor pencil, the color becomes runny because it is actually a paint. You may want to practice drawing detailed eyebrows on paper and then sealing them before you attempt it on your doll. When you are ready, use the following technique to seal the eyebrows before moving on to the rest of the face.

Dip the tip of your small paintbrush into the matte sealer. Ever so lightly dot the sealer along the entire brow line and then quickly run your brush ONCE through. Leave it alone after that! Give the eyebrow 15 minutes to dry completely before you seal it again. The second time use a very light hand and apply one more coat of sealer just running the brush through the brow area one time. Again, let it dry completely and then add one last coat in the same manner just to be safe.

Sealing the eyebrows.

You must immediately seal any areas created with watercolor pencils so that they do not smear and run on the doll. Even the oil on your fingertips can change watercolor pencil marks on your doll into liquid that will run and ruin your doll. You must use the technique that I described above so that you will not ruin the detail that you drew onto your doll. Remember, the moment the watercolor pencil gets wet, it runs. If you don't seal your work carefully, you will lose the detail that you've drawn. This does not happen with paint, so if you're using paint, just seal as normal once the paint is fully dry. Your doll's eyebrows should look similar to those shown here when you are done painting and sealing.

Painted, sealed eyebrows.

When all three coats of sealer have been applied to both eyebrows and the area has dried completely you are ready to move onto the eyes.

REPAINT REALISTIC EYES

*Eye Makeup

You are now ready to give your doll gorgeous eyes. When I say realistic eyes, I mean the makeup and lashes that adorn them as well. The lashes will be applied after the entire face is done, but you must pay attention to lower lashes and the upper lash line as you repaint the eye areas. So keep that in mind.

For the purposes of explaining the techniques for this book, I think starting from right under the eyebrow, working down to the lower lashes is easiest.

When you think about the brow bone, the crease, and the eyelid of an actual eye, the usual cosmetic application goes on in three shades: the middle shade on the lid, the darkest shade in the crease and the lightest shade on the brow bone. Using that rule, apply color to your doll in basically the same manner except when using really harsh eye colors such as purple or blue. For those colors, it is best not to bring the color up as high as the brow bone as it gives your doll a very dated cosmetic look unless it is the sheerest wash of color. For the purpose of this book, I kept my gorgeous redhead in neutral tones of beige and brown with full red lips and a bronze blush. I stuck with the norm and went for mesmerizing emerald eyes as well. Now let's begin!

Before doing anything else, you must mix 3 shades of brown paint. You can either do this by mixing the earthy colors that were described in Chapter 1 with the color wheel, or you can mix your umber shade with white to make it lighter. Either way will work. Always add water to smooth out the paints before you mix. Separate sections of paint and apply water with your brush before mixing and painting – ALWAYS! Once you create each shade, divide it in half using only one portion to create the next lightest shade.

The darkest brown shade will be used for the crease and to line under the eye. It is the original brown shade that you mix or the umber shade straight out of the tube.

Original brown and brown mixed with white (second shade).

The middle shade is used on the lid and to shade under the eye. This is your original mixed shade combined with white or your original umber shade right from the tube combined with white. Use your judgement to discern how much white to add. It is best to add the white a little at a time. You don't want the light shade to appear chalky.

Second shade mixed with blending medium to create third shade (lightest).

The lightest shade is used as a color wash for the entire area when you begin painting and as a highlight for the brow bone. It will be your middle shade combined with acrylic blending medium until it is a cloudy, light color with a barely-there tint of color. Now that you have the colors that you need, you can begin painting!

Look at your doll and see where you drew the charcoal eyeliner line in the last chapter. Start beneath that line, adding a thin layer of the color wash to the lid. Don't paint over the line that you sketched to represent the crease so that you can see the guide when you paint that part later. Continue above the pencil line up to the brow bone right under the eyelid. The wash should just give the slightest hint of color and give you an even work surface to apply the other colors.

Using third shade of mixed brown as a color wash from lid to brow-bone.

Remember that the acrylic paint from the tube dries quickly. Feel free to mix it with water so that you get a nice, smooth flow of paint each time you touch the brush to the doll's face. If you don't apply the paint in thin layers, you will get goopy, splotchy paint that will not dry properly and will probably peel off. Applying in layers is a lengthy process, but it's one that works and seasoned artists implement it for a very good reason. Wait for the color wash to dry completely (at least 10 minutes) before continuing. Do not seal at this point, but be careful not to handle the painted area.

Moisten your darkest shade now with water if necessary. Roll your paintbrush in the paint to get the thinnest, sharpest point on your brush before applying to the doll's face. Following the natural crease of the human eye in our picture, paint in the crease.

Using original brown shade to paint in eye creases.

From this point it is up to you how to further accentuate the doll's eye. You can wing the color out to the sides to give her a more dramatic look. Or you can take some of the lid shade and make it a bit darker and blend it into the crease, bringing it above the crease to give the eye a bit more depth. Use some blending medium on the brush to make the paint easier to work with and more "blend-able" giving the illusion of real makeup rather than leaving harsh paint lines where different colors meet. I kept the doll's face simple, so that it doesn't overwhelm you. In addition, it allows you to see each section of the eye more clearly.

Again, wait until this area is completely dry before moving onto the next step. This time allow it to dry for about 15 minutes because this is in essence the second coat of paint that you've applied to this area. Once that is dry, take your medium shade and apply it to the lid.

Applying second brown shade to lid.

Next, use a little black out of your tube of paint and mix with water, thinning it out. Roll the brush in the paint once again creating a sharp point on your brush. Then apply a thin line over the charcoal guide to give the upper lid an eyeliner effect.

Applying "eyeliner" with black paint.

Let the entire painted area dry for 20 minutes and seal completely with your matte acrylic sealer. Let it dry once again for 30 minutes before moving on to paint the actual eye. In the interim, do NOT throw out the brown paint. We will use it again after this section.

PAINTING THE ACTUAL EYE

*Whites

*Irises

*Pupils

*Shading

*Lower Lashes

*Inner Corners

As you might imagine, this is the trickiest part of repainting the doll's entire face. If the eyes don't look realistic, then you lose something in the translation from original screening to OOAK. In order to get the eyes right, you need to take another look at the human eye. Please refer to the photo once again to get a basic knowledge of eye shape. You may also flip back to the illustration of the human eye as well.

Notice how the whites of the eyes actually look rounded — the corners of the eyes are pinkish and the irises themselves are multi-colored. They actually look like there are thousands of tiny threads separating the colors of the iris giving the eye a truly

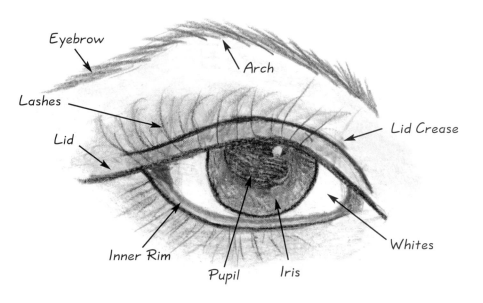

Eyebrow

Arch

Lashes

Lid

Lid Crease

Inner Rim

Pupil

Iris

Whites

unique look belonging only to this particular person. Eyes are as unique to each person as his or her thumbprint, and this is what you want to achieve on your doll. You will never be able to duplicate the beauty of a natural eye on a doll — the intricacy is just too overwhelming.

To begin, mix your paint colors.

Water down some white paint.

Mix your basic dark green color or use some from a tube of green paint.

To mix your eye color, create three shades again just as you did for the eye shadow in the shades of brown. Using your basic dark green, mix some with white for a lighter shade. Then mix some of that color with the blending medium for the lightest shade.

If you chose green for the eyes, your variations should look similar to those shown here.

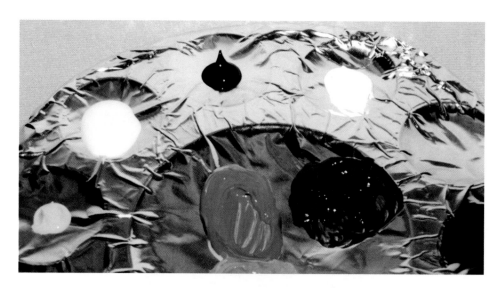

Original and second green shades.

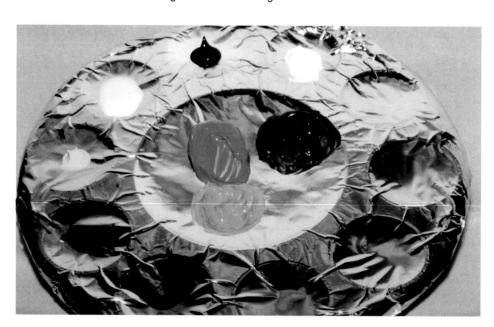

Original, second and third green shades.

Starting off with a clean brush and some very thin white paint, paint the inner whites of the eyes first. Paint AROUND your pencil guides, not over them! Follow the shapes that you sketched with the pencil. Don't worry about the lines that show around the edges of the whites. These will serve as shading as you will see later, to give added dimension to the shape of the eyes. If the color of the whites looks very thin at first, wait until the layer dries and then paint in another layer. Repeat this process until you are satisfied, always making sure your last layer of paint is dry before adding another. Let dry. Don't seal.

Painting in the whites of the eyes.

Take your darkest green color and again, roll the paintbrush in the paint to create a point. Water the paint down well so that it flows. Paint along the outer rim of the eye where you sketched the iris following the pencil marks. Let this dry completely before filling in the eye area. Again, do not seal.

Painting the rim of the iris with the original green shade (dark).

Using your medium color, apply the paint to the middle of the eye being careful not to paint over the outer edge of the dark green area that you applied first. When this is completely dry, you should have an eye with two obvious shades. Let dry completely and do not seal yet.

Filling in the iris with the second green shade (medium).

Using your lightest color green, paint in the area closest to the pupil. This is going to be the lightest color that will be emanating from around the edges of the pupil, just like in a real eye. Let dry and again, do not seal.

Using the lightest green (shade 3) paint color near the pupil.

Now, to make the eye look even more realistic, you must add dimension to it. To make them appear to be 3-dimensional rather than flat, take a complimentary color such as brown, gold or yellow and add some light to the eye. I used the primary color yellow and watered it down. I then took my brush and just swept some color to the left of the pupil, and then a thin line on the bottom right side of the pupil. I didn't paint over the iris color; I just gave two brush strokes that are very thin, but as you can see in the picture, very effective. Let dry before moving on.

Adding some yellow to the iris for realism.

Now paint in the black pupils. Some people may wonder why so many artists sell their repaints for so much money — now you can begin to see how pain staking and time consuming it really is. Artists who do their best work take the time to go the extra mile and wait for the paint to dry between each step and really give their dolls a quality repaint that not only looks good, but lasts and lasts.

Painting in the black pupils.

Now you are ready to paint in the pink corners. First, notice the gray shading around the outer whites of the eyes that you painted in. If you did your repaint correctly, you should be able to see the gray lines that you originally sketched into the eye area around the whites. This only serves to cast a little shading and make the eye look rounded and should be apparent as it is with a real human eye. If you managed to paint over those lines, fear not. You can always take a little bit of gray paint and try painting them in again with a very light touch. Now concentrate on the pink area in the corners. Take some red paint and mix with white. Now take that rose color and mix with more white so that you have pink.

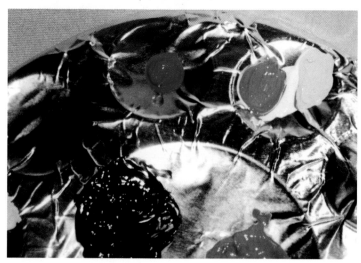

Mixed pink shades.

Roll your paintbrush in the paint and paint in a small round area of the light pink in each inner corner of the eyes outside of the range of the whites. Then take a stroke of the rose color and paint a curved line through each pink spot like this:

Painting the corners of the eyes.

The dual colors only serve to add more realism to the eye. Using some of the light pink, paint a thin line on the "inner rim" of the bottom of the eye and going towards the back. If this confuses you, look at the picture of my doll here and also look at the picture of the real human eye to get an idea.

Following the picture below, paint a pink/flesh-tone lower rim on the doll's eyes.

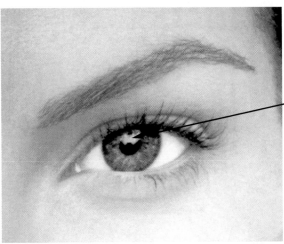

Reflection of light.

Paint in the white sparkle of light into each black pupil at this point. The eye naturally reflects light, and depending on how big or small you make your pupil, that is how much or how little white

65

paint you should be using. Also, make sure that the "light" (white paint dot) is reflected on the same side in both eyes.

Let dry completely, and then go on to seal the entire area that you just painted. I suggest sealing once, waiting 20 minutes to dry and then sealing again to be sure. You should be using gloss sealers to seal the inside of the eye area, such as the whites, pink corners and iris because on the human body, the eyes are always moist. Then, use matte sealer to seal the eye shadow and liner area. Now to shade the bottom of the eye and work on painting in those lower lashes!

Using the original brown shade saved from your previous work, wet it down again and roll your brush into it. Using the very tip of the brush, line the lower lash line leaving the area for the "inner rim" to show. This makes the eye look real.

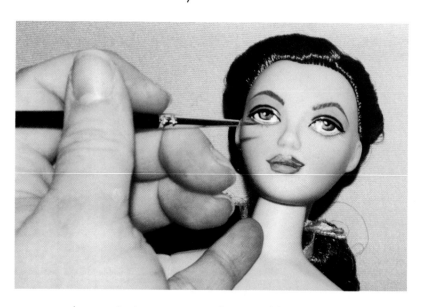

Lining the lower eyes with original brown shade.

PAINTING IN THE LOWER LASHES

I happen to love long, silky lashes so I painted plentiful lower lashes on this doll. Of course you choose your style, but either way, this part takes a steady hand. It's easy if you sketched the lashes onto your doll while sketching the features. Just remember to roll your brush in very thin, watered down paint — but not too runny —

and use a light quick stroke to follow your sketch marks. You want thin lashes not fat, sloppy ones! Seal this work with matte sealer.

Your doll's face should look something like the one pictured here.

I want to stop for a moment and just give a friendly word of advice here. There are many people out there doing this for fun and for profit. Some people adore the styles of others, and some people hate the styles of others. You are not going to be able to please everyone. Nor will your style of painting ever be exactly like anyone else's. Practice will improve your skill, but your style is all your own much like your genes. The techniques to complete a fabulous repaint are laid out for you. They are the concrete skills that you need in order to perform this craft properly. How your repaint turns out relies in your talent, how much practice you give yourself and how well you follow instruction. You may feel that your repaint turned out worse than mine, or much better than mine! Just remember that you are unique, and you should not strive to be a carbon copy of anyone else. As long as you are pleased with your work and you know that it's the best you can do, don't compare.

Now let's move on to give our doll some killer lips!

PAINTING REALISTIC LIPS

Refer back to the lip shape illustrations in the last chapter for samples and simply paint them in, shading for realism as needed.

If there is anything that you would like to change regarding the sketch, do it now. Erase the pencil and redraw them until you are satisfied. When you feel it looks good, start to repaint the lips. For this, you will need some black paint watered down, and primary red. To create the illusion that the doll's mouth has an upper and lower lip, roll your paintbrush into the black paint and paint a line between the upper and lower lips extending to the outer corners of the

upper lip. Then rinse your brush and put it into the primary red color. Line the lips. Then fill them in, painting over the black line. This, in addition to the fact that your lips have already been shaded in with the graphite pencil, will cause the red to mix ever so slightly with the tones to give you a stunning black cherry color. This makes the doll look like she just bit into a ripe berry. If the black line separating the lips disappears, paint it in again while the red lip color is still wet so it becomes blended and doesn't look like a crisp line.

Lining the lips, paint the black line separating the lips.

Filling in the lip area with color.

At this point, you can take some of the red and mix it with blending medium and apply just a touch to the middle of the lower lip to make her appear to have a pout. I just left the doll alone and will not seal her lips because I absolutely love the matte color that I ended up with on her lips. If you feel unsafe by not sealing your work, then I would suggest using matte if you want the color to be understated because it will still have somewhat of a gloss. Use the gloss sealer if you want the lip color to have a brilliant shine.

This is my doll so far. I think I will give her a nice Irish name at this point because that is where her look is leading me. Now, let's go on to give SHANNON some lush lashes and fingernail and toenail paint!

Acknowledgements: I would like to thank Christa Maher for giving me the idea to paint the black line between the lips to separate them and make the dolls' mouths look more realistic. Christa often uses this technique in her repaints. If you would like to contact Christa about her work, you can email her at cubbyscloset@hotmail.com

Chapter 6

Realistic Eyelashes, Nails and Cheek Blush

REALISTIC EYELASHES

Now it's time to give our girl some nice, flirty, lush lashes! Take your package of real women's lashes or eyelashes for dolls that you can purchase in any doll supply store, and bend the rim. This makes the eyelash more flexible.

Bending the eyelash.

Measure the lash to fit the eye of the doll and cut off any extra. Using your Scotch brand adhesive, apply a thin line to the rim

Measure, snip off extra.

of the lash and then glue onto your doll, holding upright for about 60 seconds until set. Repeat with the other eye.

Setting the lashes.

Once both lashes have been set, trim the lashes to scale for the doll's size using a sharp scissors. Remember, lashes on the inner corner of each eye are shorter than the lashes on the outer corner so cut them on an angle. If you want to curl your doll's lashes, use a heated eyelash curler. The company IGIA® makes a good one!

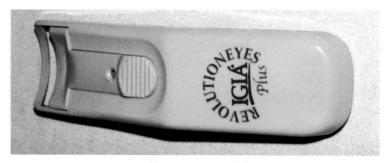

Warm temp curler.

A trick of the trade is to add some black paint just like mascara to make lashes even more lush!

Don't forget the nails! It's the little things that mean so much and often times when an artist creates a repaint on a doll, she will automatically add in painted finger and toenails. Choose whichever color you love for this, but make the fingers and toes match. It just

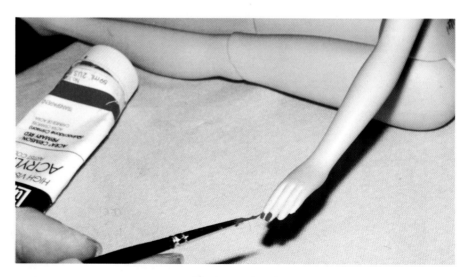

Manicure time!

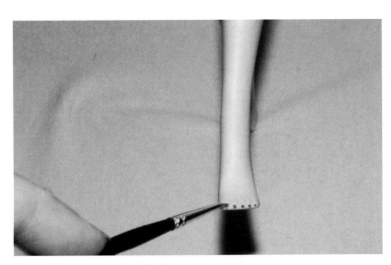

Don't forget the pedicure!

looks better, even on a real woman. Sometimes artists will have the nail color match the lip color. Or, you can go for a French manicure look, or bold color on the toes and neutrals on the fingers. Don't paint a doll's nails something you wouldn't wear yourself unless it adds to a theme or an already funky repaint!

ADDING EXTRAS

Now is the time to add some extras such as beauty marks, moles, etc. — anything that you might want to add to your doll to make her look more realistic. You can also paint in the nipple area to make the doll look more realistic, as some artists do, or paint on tattoos, etc. It's all in your imagination! Just remember to seal your work when you're done! Also, you can add tiny Bhindi-like jewels to your doll. Say you're making a belly dancer and you need a jewel in the middle of her forehead. You can put that in now.

On Shannon, I applied a mole and some gorgeous freckles. They were just perfect on a red-headed, fair-skinned Irish lass. I also gave her nostrils. The following describes how to create these features.

73

MIXING MOLE AND FRECKLE COLOR

Use the color burnt sienna for the mole, watered down well. Then use half of the burnt sienna mixed with blending medium for the freckles.

Burnt Sienna tube acrylic mixed with blending medium.

APPLYING THE MOLE

Making sure the burnt sienna color is watered down well, roll your paintbrush in the paint bringing the tip of the brush to a point. Then simply touch her face leaving a nice dot of paint. There's your mole.

So pretty! Adding the "mole".

PAINTING IN THE NOSE HOLES

While you have your brush filled with the burnt sienna color, you may decide to paint in some nostrils. You will find with practice that the application of these can change the appearance of your doll dramatically. The way you place them, what angle, how big or small really affects the way your doll looks in the end, so start small and then work your way into something more dramatic until you find the look that you want.

Painted in nostrils.

APPLYING FRECKLES

As with the rest of this repaint, you are trying to mimic what occurs naturally. The more realistic you try to keep your work, the more beautiful the result will be. Freckles are not symmetrical nor consistent in color. Some are bigger than others, some darker and

A splash of facial freckles.

75

some look like coffee splotches. Also, if someone has freckles on their face, they are sure to have them somewhere else on their body. On Shannon, I gave her very light freckles across the bridge of her nose and just a splash here and there on the upper cheek area. I didn't want her to look like a little girl and the end result was fabulous. I also splashed some freckles across her upper chest, making those a little more noticeable in that some are dark and big and others are light and small. Be creative with the "extras" — you'll be pleasantly surprised at how they can breathe life into your creation.

REALISTIC CHEEK COLOR

Finally, the cheek area is the final area in our repaint, everything else that you want to do on the face must be done now, except the final shading so that handling of the doll in the facial area will be kept to a minimum.

I am going to teach you the same technique as in my first book for cheek blush. Use real women's cosmetics, but choose a powder blush that is oil free. Apply this with a woman's eye shadow brush, which is the perfect size for a doll blush brush! Start with a light hand. This technique is so easy and so wonderful because if you get too much color you can simply wipe off with water. However, just to

Applying blush.

be safe, this will stain some vinyl material so start off with a light hand and gradually intensify. You can get so many striking effects with this technique including chiseling cheekbones out and really getting a great pink blush on the apples of the cheeks. You have so much more control with this than regular paint.

You will be using oil free blush so that the oil doesn't mottle the vinyl down the road. Once you blush the cheek area to your satisfaction, lay the doll down somewhere and don't touch her again until the next day. This will give the ground pigment in the blush the chance to seep into the vinyl and stain it. If you touch it right after, the oils from your hands will mix with the pigment and cause the blush to rub off. By the next day, the blush should have set and should not be so easy to rub off unless you use soap and water to wash it off. Even so, handling of the facial area at this point is discouraged.

Your doll should look similar to the one shown here. What a beauty! Be proud! You're about to learn the final step of a good repaint—subtle shading of the facial features as a whole!

Almost finished!

Chapter 7

Shading the Facial Area for Realism

Look at the human face of anyone near you. Do you see where there are certain areas on this person's face that are shaded? This occurs naturally and should also appear to do so on your doll. However you must not overdo it should your doll come out looking odd.

Sharpen a watercolor pencil to a fine point. Use a color that is nearest to a taupe that you can find. Brown is too dark and Sienna is too red. You will have to find a happy medium, something that is light enough to look natural but dark enough to be somewhat noticeable. Remember that the human face is shadowed in certain areas.

The first place you may want to shade is under the eye area. Take your pencil and lightly work some color into the vinyl. Using a wet dip stick or makeup applicator, smudge the pencil until it's ever so light.

Shading the under eye area.

The next place you may want to shade is around the nose and the nostrils where you only want to show prominence so use a light hand to bring the shape of the nose out.

Shading the nose outline.

Perfecting the nostrils.

The third place that is good to shade is the double line above the upper lip leading to the bottom of the nose. Again, very lightly work some color into this area; then blend the color using a wet makeup swab or dip stick. Don't use a regular cotton swab for this. I am stating a dip stick or makeup applicator because they are pointy. A regular cotton swab is too fat for this work.

Shading above the lip.

Shading nose to brow (one side only).

Shading the folds of the ear.

Some people choose to shade more areas of the doll than others. More areas that can be shaded for realism are the ear folds, the cheek lines (when a person smiles) and the area on the upper side of the nose near where the eyebrow begins. To make these shadings work you must be a truly gifted artist because if you don't do it right, it will make the doll look multicolored. So if you are unsure, practice first on a rescue doll until you become more secure in the application of your techniques.

Use a very light hand to seal this shading work. Since you are using watercolor pencil to do this you must seal because the pencil will smudge and stain the vinyl. Use a very thin size 0 brush dipped in matte sealer and stay inside the lines. Do not EVER seal a doll's entire face. It makes the doll look ghoulish!

Here is what my completely repainted, shaded and sealed doll looks like! Yours should look similar. Congratulations on a job well done! Remember, practice makes perfect! Now is the time you should be honing your skills so practice! Practice! And be very proud of what you've just managed to accomplish!

Completed repaint.

Now, be prepared to be amazed even further when you see what can be accomplished in the way of re-sculpturing with milliput paste, and a very special guest artist who is also a very dear friend! Please, read on!

Chapter 8

Sculpting with Milliput® Paste

You have just completed your first facial repaint using a variety of mediums to attain your final goal. As you become more proficient in this craft, you will begin to see that you are somewhat limited in the looks that you can achieve due to the fact that the facial mold that was used to manufacture the doll may not fit the scheme of what you want to create. Sketching, painting and similar skills can absolutely change a doll's original look, but sometimes you might want to take the next step and completely transform the mold into a new sculpt. How? By using a wonderful compound called Milliput® paste!

Milliput® paste is manufactured and primarily distributed outside of the United States, which is why a whole lot of folks have not heard of it in this country. However, with the advent of the internet, everything is so much easier to find and there are a handful of distributors scattered around this country that do sell it. You will find sources listed in the back of this book. Let's talk about Milliput® paste and exactly what it is for a few moments.

Milliput® paste is a two-part epoxy putty/modeling compound that comes in a variety of colors. The nice thing about this compound is that it adheres itself to the vinyl and will not come off easily. After a few hours it turns rock hard. Once it is dried, it can be sanded with a nail file, sanding paper or a dremmel tool. It can be drilled, painted and sealed. It is very responsive to water and can be molded and sculpted with sculpting tools to achieve the desired effect. It comes in a long thin rectangular box as you can see in the picture. The color shown is superfine white. Terra cotta is another color you will find; however, for the purpose of resculpting your fashion dolls, I would suggest the superfine white. Then mix your acrylic paints to resemble the proper flesh tone once your sculpting work is done.

When you open the Milliput®, you will see 2 lengths of material. You need to cut equal parts of these lengths and knead them together until they are mixed well and the color is uniform and streakless. Wear gloves when you are working with Milliput® because it is marked IRRITANT on the box.

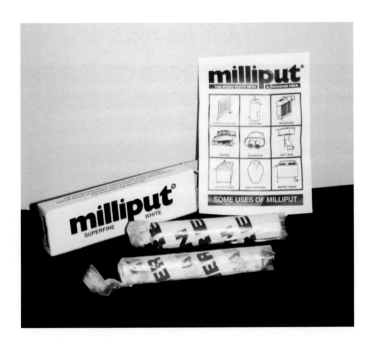

How do you actually sculpt the face with Milliput® you ask? Well, I'm glad you did! To help me with this part of the book, I have called upon a very special friend of mine who is the Milliput® man himself! During the course of my career, I have come across a fabulous artist named Juan Albuerne who has magically transformed ordinary fashion dolls into gorgeous One-of-a-kind celebrity dolls by changing the dolls' original molds with Milliput® paste. When asked about his techniques, he is an open book — that is the wonderful thing about Juan. Nothing is a secret where he is concerned and to prove that, he has agreed to help me with this chapter and bring to you the expert steps he uses in achieving a brand new facial sculpt with Milliput® paste.

TOOLS NEEDED

Superfine white Milliput® paste

Vallejo paint in Basic Skin tone and Beige Red hues

Red, blue or gray acrylic paint

Sculpting tools (learn how to make your own using
* Juan's directions below)*

File or sandpaper

Sealer

FIRST, THE TOOLS

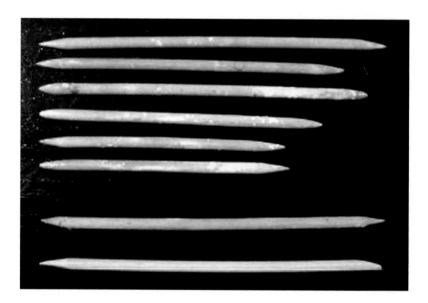

You can't always find the best tools for remodeling those tiny areas, so Juan thinks that the best way is to create your own! To make these tools, all you need is orange wood sticks and instant drying glue. For those of you who don't know what orange wood stick are, they are the little wooden sticks that you use on your cuticles that often come in nail care packs.

- Take an orange wood stick and apply some of the instant glue to the ends. (Gel glue is best, but instant drying is okay, too).
- Let it dry (if you didn't use the gel glue, repeat the process).
- Now, sand! You can sand the glued ends into any shape you want on the end of the stick: pointed, rounded, flat...the choice is yours! And when the ends wear away and you begin to lose the shape, you can always do it again. It's very fast and easy — and cheap!

PREPARING THE MILLIPUT® AND SCULPTING THE MOLD

Before you even think about beginning to sculpt your doll's face, remember, the Milliput® dries rock hard, and you are working on soft vinyl. Therefore, if there is anything that you need to do with the doll's head removed, do it BEFORE you begin applying the paste to the face. Why? Because once the paste is dried onto the face and your sculpt is completed, squeezing the vinyl on the head will cause the Milliput® to become loose and work its way off the face. Make sure the head is removed, all work is done, and the head is then replaced before sculpting takes place. To begin your work, prepare the Milliput® paste as directed above and on the box. Remember to wear gloves! Once you have some of the compound ready to use, apply a small bit to the area that you want to sculpt, whether it be the eyes, nose, lips, whatever. Begin to work on the area to shape it using your modeling tools. Add water to the Milliput® paste if it begins to get stiff in order to make sculpting and modeling easier.

Bette Davis in progress.

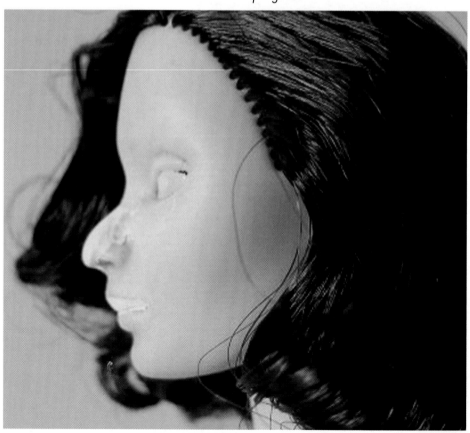

Julia Roberts in progress.

Julia Roberts completed.

In order to create "Bette Davis," Juan had to remake the upper lip. Perhaps the hardest part is finding out where to put the paste. Juan suggests taking some good pictures of the blank model (doll) and carefully comparing it to pictures of what you would like to recreate looking at it from all angles. Then you will know where to put the paste and how to mold it.

On Julia, the original doll needed a new nose, upper and lower lips and the chin needed to be redone. More of the same was done on Barbra and Glenn as seen in the pictures.

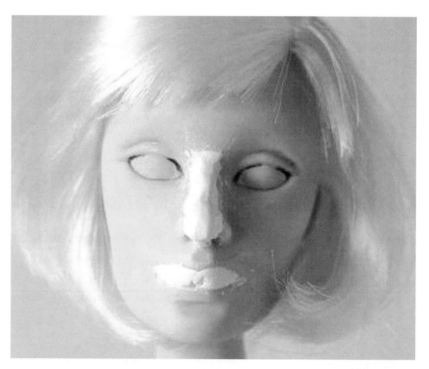

Barbra Streisand in progress.

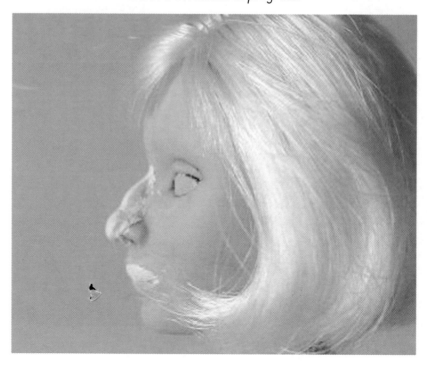

Glenn Close in progress.

    Juan advises to work with small amounts of paste and to work it carefully. Take your time sanding until you get the smoothest look. This process CANNOT be rushed! Paint it slightly and let it dry. Go over the paint as necessary to get a blended look, especially the facial areas that need flesh color to match the vinyl. You can seal your work on the eyes and lips, but do not seal the flesh-colored areas such as the forehead, cheeks, chin, and nose. The majority of the matte sealers still leave behind somewhat of a shine and it makes the doll look very peculiar. However, if you are willing to try this technique, Juan has found a way to be able to seal ALL areas and have it look great! Be sure to follow this technique exactly so as to not have a very shiny doll face:

Using Windsor & Newton™ matte sealer, which is the most matte available, Juan applies the sealer with a FLAT paintbrush that has previously been wet down with water, not soaked, just dampened. He then applies the sealer to the face. Juan agrees that this technique takes some practice and also states that if you don't dare attempt it, just leave the area unsealed!

HOW TO MIX FLESH TONE PAINT

Juan always seems to get a perfect match on his gorgeous dolls! When I asked him what he uses to achieve that flesh tone color, he told me that he always uses Vallejo® paint and mixes "Basic Skin

Above: Bette Davis.

Right: Julia Roberts.

Left: Glenn Close.

Below: Barbra Streisand.

tone" and "Beige Red" hues as the base. Then, depending on the doll that he's using, he adds either red, blue or even gray to the color to make that perfect match. Again, as with everything, this process takes patience and practice to master, but with the help of Juan Albuerne, we can all become fabulous sculptors! As you can see, his beauties are fabulous and he is a magnificent artist!

Thank you Juan for sharing your techniques and your secrets to achieving such gorgeous celebrity dolls with us!

If you are interested in contacting Juan, you can email him at jualbu@asturvia.cajastur.es or, if you are interested in seeing more of his work, his website URL is www.juanalbuerne.com.

Chapter 9

Specialty Painting

Sometimes an artist gets in a mood. It can be a zany mood, a deep mood, a mysterious mood, a playful mood. Perhaps the greatest thing about this form of artistic expression is that the possibilities of expressing any mood are virtually endless. During the course of my career, I've often done very original freehand artwork on my dolls based on my many moods. Who says that you have to like needles to be a tattoo artist? With a thin paintbrush, a steady hand, and maybe a magnifying glass (depending on how well your eyesight is) you can reproduce virtually any tattoo piece onto a doll in doll scale. I once created a Wendy O' Williams doll and replicated her rose and thorn tattoo right down to the lettering of the quote that went with it. It was what really set the doll apart from any of the others created in her likeness. Aside from painting tattoos onto your doll, there is so much more that you could do. Since this book is about facial repainting, I will go into the creation of beautiful, mysterious, mystical masques that are hand-painted directly onto the dolls' faces and adorned with items such as feathers, rhinestones, glitter, etc.

I remember when I was working on my very first "gothic" doll. I wanted to make her into a gorgeous princess of darkness, but her fabulously attractive face wasn't working for the mysterious, dark persona that I wanted the doll to take on. All of a sudden my paintbrush, dipped in black paint, was taking on a life of its own and before I knew it, my brush was painting black paint onto the doll's face! Here is a picture of the way it turned out.

Nadia Princess of Darkness c. 2000.

TOOLS

Size 0 paintbrush

Acrylic paint in black and white

Matte sealer

1 rhinestone, color and shape of your choice

Water

Scotch® brand adhesive glue

Magnifier (optional, shown right)

Water-based liquid eyeliner in

   black or gray (shown below)

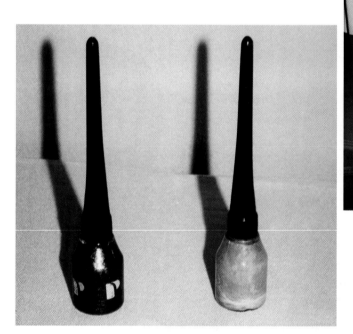

Table mounted magnifier.

Water based liquid eyeliners.

The reason that I stated the last tool, water based liquid eyeliner, is because when you are outlining the design onto your doll, you don't want to do it with paint even if you sketched it out on paper first. Using your eyeliner, draw the design of the masque free hand onto the doll's face. If you are not satisfied with something, you can simply wipe it off and begin again until you get it right. When you get it right, dip your brush in the paint and fill in the shape with color. Then you can start adorning. In this case, the base color was black with curls around to the sides of the head and eyeholes shaped like a cat masque. There were two tendrils that reach up to her forehead that "hug" an aquamarine rhinestone that was glued onto her forehead.

Once the masque is ready to be decorated, dip your paintbrush into white paint and simply dot all around the edges. You will be surprised, as I was, to see the kind of dimension and texture this brings to your doll. It's amazing. Once you are certain that the paint is dry, seal it with matte sealer.

Once you get used to drawing masques onto your doll freehand, there are so many things you can do. I once did a line of butterfly dolls, gothic dolls and fantasy pieces that included facial masques in all different designs and colors. Look in the gallery to see some of these pieces. There's no reason why you can't duplicate them onto some of your dolls!

FACIAL EXPRESSIONS

I would like to take this final note to explain the importance of facial expression. This is something that I didn't understand for a time. When I was first starting, I tried to convey certain moods and emotions onto my dolls' faces and kept coming up with the same stiff look. When I finally studied the real face and realized that all the muscles work in sync to create the outcome, I also realized that I would have to convey that through drawing, sketching, shading and painting onto my dolls' faces. When you gain more experience and confidence, try sketching in moods onto different dolls while in the sketch mode of your creation. Remember that the eyebrows, the eyes, the lines around the mouth and the lips work together to convey the message. You can't have sad, downcast eyes with a full smiling mouth or weepy knitted eyebrows with a smirk on the mouth. The face must carry the mood you are trying to convey from top to bottom. Take a look at some of the pictures of facial expression that I have managed to capture on four of my past Gene® doll creations in the gallery section of the book next, and enjoy!

95

Chapter 10

Gallery of Faces

Here is a gallery of some of the past faces I have painted. Please enjoy, and then flip ahead for a source referral for everything you may need to purchase to create the looks shown in this book!

These are the dolls with the hand-painted masques that I was describing to you in the previous chapter.

"La Farfalla"

Here are some of my more expressive faces, again trying to convey the mood from top of the face to the bottom, in sync.

Jennifer Lopez as "Catherine" in the movie *The Cell*. Notice the one arched eyebrow, the slanted narrower eyes and the side smirk she's wearing. The expression is uniform all through the face.

Gene® as Zsa Zsa Gabor. Notice the half-closed, heavy lidded eyes and pouty mouth.

Left: "Weeping Willow." She is the epitome of a woman who is on the verge of tears. From her sad, knitted eyebrows to her downcast eyes and lips that appear on the verge of trembling, you just know her heart is broken!

Below: This whimsical take on a 1940's "Dame" is very much like the "Jessica Rabbit" character. Notice the very high arched eyebrows and the stern yet sexy mouth.

Here are some extra pictures of repaints that I've done in the past for your enjoyment!

Top to bottom:

"Autum"

"Paradise Found Centaur"

"Midnight Waters Mermaid"

"Lara" from *Dr. Zhivago*
(formerly Emerald Snow)

"Mystic Blue Mermaid"

Top to bottom:

"Catra"

"Night Shadow Centaur"

"Serena the Mischievous Sprite"

Top to bottom:

"Bordeaux Fantasy Sprite"

"Gaia: Goddess of the Earth"

"Sue Catwoman"

103

Top to bottom:

"Nancy Spungen"

"Madonna circa 1985"

"Sabrina" created for a magazine column of mine

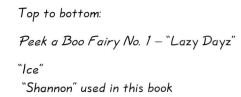

Top to bottom:

Peek a Boo Fairy No. 1 – "Lazy Dayz"

"Ice"
 "Shannon" used in this book

"Devon"

"New York Doll"

"Cleopatra

"Maxi"

"Princess Diana"   "Mystic Waters"

Sources

Listed here are some of the most reputable retailers and wholesalers that you will find on or off the internet for the materials shown throughout this book. These businesses have either been used by myself, or recommended to me through members of my Yahoo™ support group. Enjoy!

Brushes, palettes, acrylic paints, sealer, blending medium, graphite pencils and charcoal pencils among other fabulous, quality art supplies:

Dick Blick Art Materials
PO Box 1267
Galesburg, IL 61402-1267
Orders: 1-800-447-8192
Customer Service: 1-800-723-2787
Product Information:
1-800-933-2543
Website Info: www.dickblick.com

Pearl Art, Craft & Graphic
Discount Centers
308 Canal Street
New York, NY 10013
1-800-451- PEARL
Website Info: www.pearlpaint.com

Utretcht Art Supplies
1-800-223-9132
Website Info: www.utrecht.com
(ordering products, clearance and special items)
(These folks have various locations all across the US. Call the toll free number to request a catalogue.)

Liquitex® and Acra® are registered to the Binny & Smith Corp.
1100 Church Lane
Easton, PA 18044-0431
Answer Line: 1-888-4ACRYLIC or 1-888-445-4278
Website Info: www.liquitex.com

Faux eyelashes, hair for eyelash reroots and a wealth of supplies for your dolls including things like airbrushes, nail files, nail polish remover, buffing blocks, cotton balls, orange wood sticks, eye cotton swabs, makeup wedges, etc.

Sally Beauty Supply – these people only list a website, but they have a store locator online and international locations available.
www.sallybeauty.com

You can find most of the items listed above including the Scotch® brand adhesive, rhinestones, bhindi jewelry, temporary tattoos and other facial decorations at:

Genovese Drugs/Eckerd Stores:
www.eckerd.com - ordering online available

Vallejo® Acrylic Paint
www.hobby-workshop.com

Other craft stores that specialize in sewing necessities and other wonderful things you can use on your dolls:

Joanne Fabrics Online
www.joannfabrics.com

Michael's Craft Stores
www.michaels.com

Wal-Mart
www.walmart.com

Milliput® Paste
www.milliput.com
(Informative Website tells you all about the product and has a locator that will give you contact information on the nearest representative or dealer to you.)

Lastly, how could we forget the doll dealers? Please find the best in the business to follow (based on price, shipping charges and customer service):

North Shore Collectables
480 Main Street
Glen Ellyn, IL 60137
630-858-9191
www.northshorecollectables.com
(This place has wonderful sales on the collectible dolls for those who want to work on higher quality dolls without spending a fortune.)

Paul David World of Dolls
810 Blockwater Road
Chillicothe, OH 45601
www.MiKelman.com
(This place has excellent prices on dolls such as Candi™, Charisse™, Alyssa™, etc.)

Browns Gallery
82 Sandiford Drive #17
Stouffville, Ontario L4A 7X5
Canada
www.brownsgallery.net
(This place has some great buys on Gene® from time to time.)

Pat's Potpourri – Dolls and Shoes
http://pats_potpourri.tripod.com
(This place is an authorized dealer for Candi™, Jade™, Alysa™ and Janai™ dolls from Integrity Toys® and has a wide variety of Kingstate® shoes to offer for dolls of various sizes.

DON'T FORGET! For some of the hard to find items and a large selection of vintage dolls and heads to mix and match for your creations, the world's largest flea market online is the best place to begin!

www.ebay.com

Please visit me on the web!
www.creatingfashiondolls.50megs.com
Sign up to join my artist support group on Yahoo™, the Artists of OOAK at: www.yahoogroups.com/group/artistsofooak

If you wish to send me your questions, comments and suggestions for future books please email me at: dollusions@aol.com

109

Artist
Afterword

Hello again. I hope you have enjoyed reading <u>Creating Fashion Dolls: A Step-by Step Guide to Face Repainting</u>. Now, go through it again and actually do the step by step and practice! Even if you don't think so, I'm sure you will have a true beauty on your hands when you are done. Anything that is created with the heart, mind and hands is something of value and beauty.

I wanted to say a few closing words — words to leave you with and to make you think and realize some things that might not have been evident up to this point. First and most importantly, the intent of my book is to encourage you to develop the proper skills that are needed to hone your own artistic talent. You are only limited to your own talent and imagination. Anything worth doing is worth doing well, and anything that you do well is certainly something to be proud of.

When I created the showgirl for <u>Creating Fashion Dolls A Step-by-Step Guide to One-of-a-Kind Fashion Dolls</u>, the intent was to show you how incredibly easy it is to design an entire OOAK fashion doll from scratch with little to no experience in the field. What resulted was an email box that was inundated with pictures of other aspiring artists' creations — dolls that were inspired by my example. Let me tell you to say the least, they were ALL phenomenal. The funny part was that none of them looked like mine! That was the whole point of that book.

The same holds true for this book. While the repaint in <u>Creating Fashion Dolls: A Step-by Step Guide to One-of a-Kind Fashion Dolls</u> was a very easy trace-over-the-original-screening exercise in technique, this book delves deeper into the world of repainting a doll's face and giving her more realistic features. It covers everything that you need to know about repainting and facial structure, as well as paints and all the other materials that you should have on hand to practice this art. I can guarantee that if a thousand people practice my step by step instructional from this book, and you line the finished dolls up on a table, no two of them will look exactly alike, or exactly like mine for that matter. As I said earlier: Nobody's styles are alike. Even with the same lesson nobody will create the same way.

These books are meant to take your imagination to new heights – to make that proverbial light bulb go off in your head and say "whoa! THAT'S how they do that!" and then come up with your own ideas for using that technique! These books are also the only one of their kind on the market and therefore they are truly OOAK in themselves. I hope that both will continue to teach and inspire you for many years to come. Even after you become a truly fabulous designer and repaint artist.

I would also like to take this opportunity to address those of you who wish to pursue this craft and make your designs visible to the general public. Those who do this for a hobby have found a wonderful outlet to explore creativity in almost every form. From sketching and drawing, to painting, to costume and fashion design and hair styling – it is a very relaxing, satisfying and productive craft. I often feel exhausted in a good way once I'm done with a design and I'm looking at the finished product. However, those who wish to make money in this field must know a few things right off.

Your repaint could be absolutely gorgeous in person, but unless you are going to a doll show or somewhere to sell your dolls in person, the image may become distorted or not as attractive as it could be if you are using inferior camera equipment. The internet has been very good to me and has afforded me many customers who have bought my dolls throughout the years that I've been creating, but the first thing that I did was to go out and invest in a good digital camera. There are books on lighting and backgrounds and camera angles, etc that you should really familiarize yourself with if you are not up to paying the fees of professional photographers for your work. Presentation in person and in digital form means EVERYTHING.

With that said, I would like to close on another piece of advice. This is going to affect each one of you in a different way because it is very personal, but I realized that it is very important for aspiring artists who want to make money from this craft to know this going in. There are many wonderful people who are quite willing to help, and share and make friends in this inspiring hobby – however there are those that are also very petty and jealous. Be aware that those that spout venom are the ones who are usually talentless and will do anything to make someone feel inferior. Any time an artist creates something – and please listen to this because it's very important and very true – and puts it out for general consumption, he is bound to be reviewed by bad critics. It is part of developing a thick skin and not giving up on yourself or your talents. I am no exception. I have fallen victim in the past myself. Of course I do consider myself a professional and somewhat successful, but if I had listened to those jealous, petty people who said mean, rotten things, I would have short changed myself out of a very rewarding career. I don't say that this will ever happen to you, but if it does, you cannot let it get to you. You have to turn the other cheek and while it is easier said than done, it CAN and MUST be done. If you are ever faced with a situation where you are being criticized, take it for what it is worth and if YOU think that you could use the suggestions, then use them and use them wisely. Then get past it and move on.

Just remember, as long as you do what you love and do it well you will be just fine. If you are looking for somewhere fun and safe to come to make friends and share your questions, ideas, suggestions and talents, join my Yahoo™ group – the URL is in the "sources" chapter! I wish you good luck in all your endeavors. Untill next time! Take care!

If you would like to email me, you can reach me at: dollusions@aol.com.

If you would like to order additional copies of this book that will be autographed personally to you or the person of your choice, please contact me via email stated above or look for my dutch auctions on ebay™ under the seller ID dollusions.

Watch for future books in this series to come! Thank you for your interest and as always, happy creating!

~Sabrina Guidice